The Most Frequently Asked Questions About Gymnastics

The Most Frequently Asked Questions About Gymnastics

Karen M. Goeller

Common Questions...

Thousands of people are involved in the sport of gymnastics and there are thousands involved only as spectators. The athletes, coaches, parents, and spectators and many have questions.

This book is a compilation of some of the questions Karen personally has been asked. Many of the parents of athletes have questions and concerns regarding their children's training and experiences.

The purpose of this book is to help answer some of the questions about the sport. With this book we hope to enlighten you on some important points of interest you may or may not have thought about regarding this sport.

Please keep in mind when reading through this book that these answers are Karen's opinion based on her experiences; there may be several answers or opinions to many of these questions.

Topics

Skills and Events

Lucinda Asks
Subject: Gym skills
Question: Hi - I am going to America in the summer to teach gymnastics (I'm from England) but some of the skills are called different things in the US and UK so I am bit confused. If you could tell me what these next skills mean then that'd be brilliant.
Beam - scale, stick position
Bars - pullover, 180 degree turn, single leg cut over, straddle sole circle dismount
Thanks in advance!

Hello Lucinda,

Beam scale is balancing on one leg while the other is in a high position behind body, split of the legs if possible. Stick position could be a variety of things...stick a landing? Or stick a flight series? It is usually a tight finish position.

On bars, a pullover is a pull up and then the gymnast brings her hips to the bar while her legs go over the bar. She ends up in a front support. It is a beginner skill.

180 means a half turn or pirouette.

Single leg cut over is when the gymnast starts in a front support and brings one leg up and over the bar to finish with one leg in front of bar while sitting on back of thigh of the front leg.

Straddle sole circle dismount...gymnast starts with hands and feet on bar, swings down and releases bar once the buttocks passes the bar base. Gymnast releases feet first and then releases hands in order to land on her feet.

You are welcome to order my book of drills. It has over 75 drills and conditioning exercises with simple, but useful illustrations. www.gymcoach.sport.new.net

Megan M. Asks:
Subject: Level 8 Skills, Drills, Conditioning
Question: Dear Karen,
Hi! I am thirteen years old and competed level 8 this past season. If you have any ideas for vaults I should perform, please let me know. Currently, I do front fronts and tzukaharas. Do you know any drills for these skills or conditioning for the muscles needed to perform these vaults? Also, if you know any conditioning, skills, and/or drills that all advanced gymnasts should do, please tell me about that too. My strength is vault and my weakness probably is bars, although bars is my favorite event. I am a powerful gymnast, not too graceful. Thank you very much, and please reply back,
Again thanks,
Meg

Hello Meg,

Without knowing you or seeing your vaults I cannot tell you which ones to perform. That would be something your coach should do.

Doing running drills will help any vault along with upper body plyometric drills. You are welcome to email me directly if you would like to order my book of drills and conditioning, but your coach should really be designing your training program for safety reasons.

Katie Asks
Subject: back handsprings
Question: My coaches have tried to help me several times, but I was wondering if you had any different advice. I am working on connecting two back handsprings on beam. I have no problem with one, but when it comes to the second one, I am afraid to just leave my arms up and go. I know I can do it, but I just have a tendency to bring my arms down and pause before the second one. Any suggestions on getting over the fear?
Thanks!!

Hello Katie,

Try connecting several sets of 4 back handspring step-outs on floor. Remember what the third and fourth feel like.

Try placing a folded panel mat the long way at the end of a low beam as if to extend the length of the beam. Do your first back handspring on the beam, but connect another one so that you end up actually doing the second onto the panel mat.

Also try handstand step down to back handspring.
Remember, the more you do, the more comfortable you will be with this flight series.

Barb Asks
Subject: press handstands
Question: Hey Karen,
I need help with press handstands. Do you have any drills or conditioning that I can do? Thanks!!!!
Hello Barb,

I have several drills for press handstands!
Here are a few ...

Press Lean...
1. Stand with hands flat on floor in front of body and legs in straddle
2. Shift weight from feet to hands and hold weight on hands while leaning forward and getting comfortable in pressing position.
3. Hold at least 10 seconds each time.

Press Lean, Lift One Leg...
1. Perform the Press Lean and while all of the body weight is on the hands, lift one leg three to six inches from floor.
2. Hold this position at least 10 seconds before repeating with other leg.

Press Lean Lift to Straddle Through...
1. Perform the Press Lean and lift both legs approximately six inches from floor.
2. Then straddle through to straddle L Position and hold. Gymnast can also press back up half way, similar to the Lift Feet/Lift Butt Drill.
3. Sit on floor in a straddle position.
4. Place hands on floor in front of body.

5. Lift feet and legs off floor.
6. Keep feet and legs off floor and lift buttocks up.
7. Try to lift buttocks higher than head. (First half of a press handstand)
8. Repeat several times.

You are welcome to e-mail me directly for information regarding my drills book.

Karine Asks
Subject: 1/4 turn back handsprings on beam
Question: I would really like to compete in level 8 a quarter turn back handspring on beam. I don't know if USAG rules will let me as a level 8. What is the skill worth? My coach thinks a D or an E, but I don't think he's right. Please write back as soon as possible. Basically I have two questions.
What is the skill value?
Can I do it as a level 8?
Thank you,
Karine

Hello,

I am not sure of the value. My guess would be it is a B or C. You may also want to stick with B valued skills for flight and train and compete C jumps and leaps.

You might be wise to get the FIG book to learn the value of skills.

Jong Asks
Subject: Correcting My Round-Off
Question: Hello

13

I've been learning tumbling for about a year now (FYI I'm 28 yrs old) recreationally. Recently, my coach mentioned my feet stay apart too long prior to snap-down during round-off. Now I'm so worried about getting my round-off right that it's affecting back hand springs (for example, I can't throw 3 bhs in a series and not setting for my tuck). I feel like my coach never told me that now. But I did notice my legs apart and it does seem to slow me down. Do you have any suggestions/drills to solve this problem? It's probably 90% mental but I would love to hear your expert opinions on this. Just bothers me to think that I can't do what I used to be able to. Thanks in advance.

Hello,

A good round-off takes a long time to develop.

1. Try getting your feet together on the way up rather than just before you land.
2. Also try reaching further and straighter; that usually helps gymnasts tumble out of it.
3. Another thought; try tucking your buttocks under and lifting your chest as you are standing up out of the round-off.

Without seeing it I can't give you more specific help.

Make sure you are doing appropriate conditioning. Without power and speed, your muscles just will not perform as well.

You can send me a very short video of skills to look at. I will write recommendations and give suggestions to help make your skills more technically correct. If you or any of your fellow athletes are interested in a video evaluation, please write to me directly.

Jamie G Asks
Subject: Safety
*Question: Hi, I am a coach at a gym in NJ. For the past 6 years we have been in a small (2,200 sq. ft) gym. We are about to move into our new 8,800 sq. ft gym. I know it is small compared to other gyms but it is huge for us. In the old gym we did not have a full size FX or any pits. Now we have 24 * 30 ft loose foam pit. We have a recessed tumbling strip, tumble-trak, trampoline and single rail all that have access to the pit. 95 % of our students have never even seen a pit before much less been in one and I know the first thing they are going to want to do is dive in.*
To avoid injuries I am planning a Safety Day lesson plan for our first week. Can you give me some ideas of drills that I can use? I am creating 3 different plans (Pre-school, Rec and Team). Any suggestions you have would be great.
Thanks
Jamie

Hello,

Never land on your head, never land on your stomach, try not to land feet first.

The safest landing is "feet to seat." Many gyms allow their gymnasts to land in several positions and their athletes go home with injuries.

It may be wise to visit another gym, one with a good reputation, to see how they use their pit. IGC is a great place for pit training!

David Asks
Subject: conditioning program
Question: hello. I'm a 22 year-old gymnast who competes at the college level. The only exercise I get is gymnastics, so I try to put plenty of time into it. I am currently interested in getting an iron cross, planche, and v-sit, but understand I need general strength work too. I have good flexibility. I should also mention that I train and compete all around. Can you recommend a conditioning program for me?
Thank you very much for your time!

Hello David,

Here are a few exercises that will help.

Wall Climbs (for shoulder strength)
1. Stand with back close to padded wall.
2. Place hands on floor/mat approximately 1-2 feet from wall.
3. Place feet on wall.
4. After you are strong enough in that position...
5. Simultaneously walk hands in towards wall and feet up wall towards ceiling until forehead touches wall and shoulders touch ears.
6. Walk back out, remaining very tight.
7. Walk in and out several times in a row.
8. Once this is mastered, perform shoulder shrugs in the handstand position before rolling or walking back out.

Also try to go from handstand to planche positions several times is a row from the same wall climb position.

Take precautions…the mat must be secured against wall and the inexperienced gymnast must be watched closely to prevent falling into arched position against wall.

Octagon Rocks (for shoulder and chest strength)
1. Place hands on floor or floor bar.
2. Place pointed feet and shins on octagon/barrel.
3. While keeping arms straight, body tight and hollow, and legs on octagon, rock forward and backward.
4. Rock from ankles to knees, keeping thighs from touching octagon.

Go from stretched shoulder to planche position and then return to stretched shoulder position.

The iron-cross; have someone spot you for several each week. The coach/teammate can spot less each time. They just hold your ankles and help you slower lower to the position as well as rise back up from the position.

You can also do many wide grip pull ups pulling your head in front of and behind the bar.

Amy J Asks
Subject: Bars Complex
Question: I am working on a bars complex for our level 4,5 and 6 kids for the summer. We have 2 sets of bars, a strap bar, low single bar, floor bar and high bar over a pit to work with and about 25 kids. I am a little overwhelmed at where to start this process. What skills are needed and what drills to

help them all progress. Also, any conditioning that would help them to improve overall. Thank you for your help!
Amy

Hello Amy,

Your question is extremely involved. If you would like me to design your training program, I would need to charge a fee. In order to find out what skills are needed you should purchase the compulsory book from USA Gymnastics.

Remember, the sport is not only about what skills are needed. In order to train the gymnasts properly with the least amount of injury, they must be strong and flexible. The gymnasts must be able to connect skills on bars, so train with that in mind.

Below are a few drills.

Band Kips
1. Wrap a therapy band or surgical tubing around the base of very sturdy equipment such as the beam, vault, or bar base.
2. Lie on back and grasp the band or surgical tubing. The head should be closer to the base than the feet. Bend knees.
3. Holding the band very tight, while keeping the arms straight and close to body, pull band toward the ceiling and then down toward the thighs.
4. Return the band slowly using the same direction, toward the ceiling then toward the base.
This should simulate the upper body performing a kip on the bars.

Band Casts
1. Wrap a therapy band or surgical tubing around the base of very sturdy equipment such as the beam, vault, or bar base.
2. Lie on back and grasp the band or surgical tubing. The feet should be closer to the base than the head. Bend knees.
3. Holding the band very tight, while keeping the arms straight and close to body, pull band from the thighs toward the ceiling and then up toward the head.
4. Return the band slowly using the same direction, toward the ceiling then down toward the base/thighs.

This should simulate the upper body performing a cast to handstand on the bars.

Octagon glides and toes to bar
1. Grasp bar, holding hollow and slightly piked position. Place feet on octagon or barrel.
2. Swing/glide forward, keeping feet on octagon and reaching an extended position three times.
3. At the end of the third glide, while extended, quickly bring ankles/toes to bar.

You may also benefit from going to camps and watching the more experienced coaches as well as visiting other clubs and observing.

Good Luck in your training and have a great day!

Anon Asks
Subject: Bars
Question: Do you have any advice on blind changes?

Thanks!

Hello

1. Make sure your giant swings are strong and tight.
2. Blind changes usually work well if the gymnast completely extends once her feet pass the low bar.
3. It is also very important to tap late and turn simultaneously.
4. I used to tell my gymnasts to think of a candlestick and a half turn.
5. Keeping the head in and ear on the shoulder are very helpful.

Gaylynn Asks
Subject: most effective drill
Question: What is, in your opinion, the most effective drill for the cast-to-hand on bars and on average how long should it take to acquire this skill?

Also, when considering Gym-acro series for level 7 floor, do aerial cartwheels, valdez, and front-walkovers constitute acro?

Hello,

You may find my drills book to be very useful. It was written with the developmental gymnast in mind. Go to www.gymcoach.sport.new.net for more information.

These are only two of several specifically for cast handstands.

Cast & Hold

1. Start in a front support on bar.
2. Cast: pike and lean forward, look for knees, and then quickly and immediately kick legs back, push hips off bar, and push down on bar with upper body.
3. Gymnast must remain tight and hollow.
4. Coach can catch gymnast's shins, hold in cast position, and allow gymnast to rock forward and back as if performing the octagon rock drill previously explained.
5. Once gymnast is able to remain tight while being held in position, coach can lift gymnast up to handstand position.
6. Return the gymnast back to the bar in support position.

P-Bar Walks and Swings

1. Set up either 2 stacks of panel mats or 2 blocks, leaving enough space to walk between.
2. Place a mat on the floor between the mat stacks.
3. Keeping feet off floor, bend knees if necessary, place one hand on each stack/block.
4. Walk with hands to end of stack. Also walk backward.
5. Once mastered, remain in the center with feet off floor and supported on hands.
6. Swing lower body forward and backward, keeping arms straight and attempting to swing to handstand at top of backward swing.

You need to read through the compulsory book and code of points to learn the level 7 values and rules.

Becky H Asks
Subject:
Bars- the counterswing
Question: Do you have any suggestions for lead up drills for teaching the counterswing on bars, and, what suggestions do you have to help gymnasts eliminate that nasty tap on counterswings. (I know generally it means they are releasing too early, but what other tips can you offer?)

Hello Becky,

The best thing for you to do at this point is to go to a reputable gymnastics club several times and for several hours to observe how they work with their young athletes on bars.

Jennifer G Asks
Subject: Straddle back on bars
Question: How can I get the gymnasts to keep their legs from dragging on a straddle back. The girls are strong, flexible, and can do the skill well except for letting their heels hit the mat usually between the bars. We need every tenth we can get for Sectionals this week-end. Any help would be appreciated.

Hello Jennifer,

That is a common problem with straddle backs.

1. Make sure your athletes hip flexor muscles are extremely strong; make sure they are landing on the low bar in a controlled and correct position so the glide is easier and controlled.
2. And remind the girls to bring their toes to the bar in order to glide.
3. If they hit the handstand, tell them to slightly planche while they bring their toes to the bar to control the glide.

Without seeing the gymnast perform the skill it is difficult to give you more specific suggestions.

Allison Asks
Subject: Beam Dismounts
Question: I am a coach in need of assistance. I have a girl who is starting to learn aerial/barani dismounts on beam. I have not had a lot of experience teaching this dismount, so I was wondering if you had any advice, drills, on how to help her do this dismount.
Thank you,
Allison

Hello Allison,

Make sure your athlete pushes hard enough from her take off leg and that she is tight in the air.

It is difficult to coach a skill or make corrections without actually seeing the athlete perform it. I am available for video evaluations in cases such as this.

You are welcome to visit my home-page for further contact information. www.gymcoach.sport.new.net

Mary Asks
Subject: grips- yes or no
Question: My daughter is 9 and started in a rec. class Sept/00. She has since progressed from this to 6 and then 9 and now 12 hours of training. From the beginning she has not wanted to wear grips on the bars. She has had a few tears but seems to be toughing her hands without too much difficulty. Her coach has now said she should have grips due to her lengthened training and it would be to difficult to try and start using them at higher levels. What would you have to say about this? Also, a parent of a male gymnast told us to use mitchum
Hello Mary,

The deodorant is to prevent excessive sweating of the hands because sweaty hands can cause the athlete to slip off the bars. That is not necessary.

Every coach has a different opinion on when their athlete should start wearing grips. My athletes didn't wear them too early on because we were more concerned with their hands being too small for the grips and developing their grip/hand strength first.

Other coaches have their gymnasts wear grips from the first day. You should really listen to the coaches in your club; I am sure they have reasons for their decisions.

Catie Asks
Subject: Back Walk-Over help

Question: Hi, I was in level 4 at Paramount, but I had to quit. It's been a year since I've done gymnastics, but now I want to get my back walk-over done. I can go back into a bridge, but for some reason I have trouble kicking my legs over. Can you give me any tips as in where I should put my hands or how close my feet should be to my hands? Thank you very much.

Hello Catie,

Paramount in NJ? If so…great gym!
I would not suggest doing tumbling at home or without a coach present.

With that said…walkovers really involve shoulder position and shoulder flexibility.
If an athlete thinks about sticking her arm pits out to get her shoulders above her hands, the kicking over part is much easier and more technically correct.
It may be a good idea to see if you can return to a class at Paramount, even if it is with a different group.

Debra Asks
Subject: beam
Question: My daughter is currently finishing level four competitive gym. On the beam there are two bells toward the end. I have been given contrasting information regarding these bells.
Does the gymnast have to make it to the first bell to avoid having points deducted? What exactly do the bells signify?
Also do you possibly have a level five skills checklist?
Thanks

Hello Debra,

The first bell is the warning that the gymnast is running out of time and the second is that she is actually out of time.

I do not have a level 5 checklist, but the coaches should have everything your daughter needs, including the knowledge necessary, in order to move your daughter up to level 5.

You may also be able to find further information on the USA Gymnastics web-site.
www.usa-gymnastics.org

Jennifer Asks
Subject: Level-8 Vault
Question: I have a great group of level-7 gymnasts and this has been my first season as an optional coach. I have done lots of homework and my 7's have won two first place team trophies and we are getting ready for our state meet! I have 3 gymnasts that I have been working level-8 with but I am stuck on vault. I have been on line with USAG trying to make sure that we are working on vaults that they can compete at level-8. My problem is that I have come across information saying I can do certain vaults then I will get information saying that I can not do these vaults. Can you help me to find a level-8 vault table of vaults that I can compete in the up coming level-8 season?

Hello Jennifer,

Congratulations on your success with your level 7's! That is a great accomplishment for a new optional coach!

I have looked at my chart called " 'DEM Cards 10/00 Jr. Olympics" It states that Level 8's can do "Group 1 & 3 Vaults valued at 9.5 or less. All other vaults void event."

Make sure you have a FIG Book and try to purchase this extremely useful laminated card.

Jennifer L. Asks:
Subject: vaulting
Question: I am currently a level 5 coach in USA Gymnastics. Do you have any drills/ suggestions on how to get students to make a faster hurdle to the board, so as not to lose speed that is generated from the run? i have a couple students who have very strong running skills, but are unable to connect the run and the long jump to the board smoothly. They can get over the vault, but it is obvious that they are losing speed from the run into the jump to the board.

Thanks for your suggestions!

Hello Jennifer,

Have them do board drills without the horse.

1. Place the board on the diagonal of the 40x40 two thirds of the way down.
2. Have your gymnasts sprint (run at top speed) and pass right by the board.
3. Then have your gymnasts sprint and run right over the board without losing speed.
4. And then have them sprint and perform a straight jump on the board and land on a landing mat.

5. Alternate the three drills.

Fun with Running ...
A Crucial Skill for So Many Sports...

Since so many sports, including basketball, baseball, softball, soccer, gymnastics, and of course track and field, require good running technique, coaches must concentrate on teaching proper running technique.

Most people and often even athletes and coaches take for granted that if they can run, they are performing efficiently, but this is often not the case. Even with professional ball players, corrections can be made with running technique and\or speed. Running should be analyzed, broken down into smaller parts drills, and then taught correctly.

Foot alignment, knee lift, heel lift, arm swing, and even where the athlete is focusing should be trained individually, corrected, and practiced frequently. Perhaps during training, each portion of the run or the drills\techniques should be used as a warm up for training or for a more enjoyable experience, as relay races.

For a relay race each portion\movement of the run can be performed by a different teammate. Another idea is to have every participant in the race perform a certain portion or movement of the running technique.

A great contest idea for athletes is to use the arm swing for the run; once the correct elbow bend\angle and swing (alternate motion of forward and back) is learned, the number of arm swings per 30 seconds can be timed. Coaches must watch that the athletes keep their arms bent throughout the swing rather than bending and straightening with each swing. The "karate chop" motion is popular and may be a natural movement for some, but it is incorrect. The participant with the most correct arm swings can be the winner.

With the knee lift motion; once it is learned correctly without impact (marching in place and marching forward) and then with impact (running in place lifting knees and running forward lifting knees) the participants can race toward the finish using the knee lift motion. Of course, if the knees have not been lifted to at least hip height or even belly button height the knee lift was not performed correctly and that participant can not be the winner, especially since the race was specifically designed in order to practice using the knee lift motion for correct running technique.

The same race can be performed using the heel lift or actually the heel to buttocks (kick butt) motion. This motion should be learned separately from the knee lift motion. Once learned correctly using a march\walk and then a running in place and running forward motion, have your participant's race while using the kick buttocks motion. Remember, if the heels do not touch the buttocks each time, that participant cannot be the winner, especially since the participants were actually learning and practicing the heel lift for proper running technique.

Once both the knee lift and the heel lift have been learned and practiced, they can be combined. It takes a great deal of coordination to combine both! It is easiest explained by stating that the participant must lift one knee (right leg) and then kick the buttocks with the other foot (left). It is lift knee, kick butt. And it takes even more coordination to continue toward a finish line alternating the two techniques! It feels awkward and does take practice.

After the leg motions and arm swing are learned separately, they can be combined. Perhaps try to combine the knee lift with the arm swing or the heel lift with the arm swing. Once each leg motion can be combined with the arm swing, the participant is ready to attempt a sprint toward a finish line using all of the proper techniques. The coach must constantly observe and make useful suggestions to the athletes such as lift the knees, opposite arms, and keep the elbows bent while performing the arm swing.

You see, there is a great deal of learning and careful practice that goes into the proper running technique and eventually an efficient sprint. Just think of how many baseball players would be on base safely and how many more football players would score touchdowns if they ran just a bit faster! And how many more gymnasts would vault more successfully if every one of them would practice running technique on a regular basis.

Besides good technique, many athletes need more speed. This is not something that is improved or learned as proper technique is. And is usually is not improved within minutes or over night. One sports coach stated that anyone looking to increase their running speed should run down hill. This will force the athlete to run faster because gravity is at work. The muscles will be forced to react quicker, thanks to gravity, and eventually the athlete will be able to react this quickly on their own. Quicker reaction\movement equals a quicker run\sprint. The coach must keep the angle of the hill in mind, because if it is too steep there could be risk of injury.

So go out there and help your athletes perform better by teaching and correcting running technique. Good luck and May the force be with you!

The running drills mentioned in this article can be found in the book, "Over 100 Drills and Conditioning Exercises." It is a training manual that was written for gymnastics coaches, but is useful to physical education teachers, dance teachers, and any coach in need of running drills.

Debra Asks
Subject: blocking drills
Question: Hi, I am looking for new ideas for blocking drills for
my 5 & 6 year old pre-team girls and level 4's.
Thanks! Debra

Hello Debra,

1. First you need to see whether they can shrug their shoulders. Have them do the "I don't know" action with their shoulders, bringing their shoulders up to their ears.
2. Once that is mastered, have them do the "I don't know "action with their arms up and straight.
3. Children have the tendency of bending at their elbows rather than actually lifting/shrugging their shoulders, so watch for that.
4. After your athletes are able to perform the "I don't know" action/shrug standing up, with a tight body, and with their arms up, (fingers pointing toward the ceiling & not the wall) have them get into a handstand position.
5. Once the handstand is tight, have your athletes perform a shrug, of course with straight arms.
6. As a conditioning exercise and as a vault station have your athletes perform several shrugs in each handstand.

To help get your athlete's shoulders stronger, and improve their blocking action, introduce the following exercises and drills.

Wall Climbs
1. Stand with back close to padded wall.
2. Place hands on floor/mat approximately 1-2 feet from wall.
3. Place feet on wall.
4. After the gymnast is strong enough in that position...
5. Simultaneously walk hands in towards wall and feet up wall towards ceiling until forehead touches wall and shoulders touch ears.
6. Keeping arms straight, either walk back out, remaining very tight.
7. Or keeping arms straight, slide feet down and roll out.
8. Once this is mastered, perform shoulder shrugs in the handstand position before rolling or walking back out.

Take precautions...the mat must be secured against wall and the inexperienced gymnast must be watched closely to prevent falling into arched position against wall.

Handstand hop
1. Kick to handstand on mat.
2. Immediately hop up to folded panel mats or a springboard. (The hop is actually a very fast shrug with a tight body.)

Handstand hop and fall
1. Kick to handstand on board.
2. Immediately block/pop up to fall onto back on very soft and slightly raised mat.

Handstand, hop, hop, and fall
1. Kick to handstand on board.

2. Immediately block/pop up to a handstand on raised mat or wedge mat.
3. Immediately after first hop to handstand on raised mat, block/pop up again to fall onto back on very soft and slightly raised mat.

Once the last two drills are mastered, take them to the horse and perform them from a handspring vault.

These drills and the illustrations, along with many other drills, can be found in, "Over 75 Drills and Conditioning Exercises." For more information on that book, go to WWW.GYMCOACH.SPORT.NEW.NET.

Mental Preparation

Mary Asks
Subject: gymnastics
Question: I want to make sure that I am offering the best for my daughter. She started taking gymnastics at 18 months old and loves it and thinks about it everyday. She just made pre-team and is now 6 years old. She is also taking a ballet class once a week.

She talks about wanting to go to the Olympics but I am no expert at gymnastics and not sure if she has "what it takes" is there anyway or at what age can you see if it is there? I just want to make sure that it is something that she really wants to do and that it is not something that I want her to do. I just want her to enjoy what she is doing.
Mary

Hello Mary,

No one can tell if a child has what it takes to be an Olympian. Many children love the sport until they reach a competitive level.

Many coaches can see great physical potential in children, but none know whether a child will enjoy the extreme dedication this sport requires to compete on higher levels.

The best thing to do now is to allow your daughter to enjoy the sport, be supportive, and see where she goes.

If she competes throughout her childhood and remains happy, but does not reach the Olympics, she will be among the thousands of young girls learning the sport as well as life lessons through the sport.

There are only a handful of spots on the Olympic Team; keep that in mind.

It is easier to become a doctor or a lawyer than it is to become an Olympian. Both professions have millions of spots available while again there are only a handful of Olympic Team spots.

It is a great goal, but smaller goals should be set and achieved along the way.

Lisa C Asks
Subject: Overcoming fear on beam
Question: I have a 13 year-old daughter who just finished a year competing at Level 8. She had problems all year with going for her series on beam and it seems to be getting worse. Two other girls at the gym are having the same problem and their coach is getting nowhere with them. She told one of the other moms and me this morning that she is about to give up on them.
I was never a gymnast (and not much of an athlete) and I don't know how to help her overcome this fear. She is willing to try all kinds of new things on floor, bars and vault (and even beam) but will NOT do her series. I'm not sure what the problem is---she just says she's afraid.
Any ideas on what to do to overcome this? It's been going on for a LONG time.
Thanks for any advice you can give us.

Hello,

If the coach is going to give up then find a better coach! With that said...Many gymnasts feel overwhelmed when they are expected to perform several new skills simultaneously. Most often, this happens in the lower optional levels, when they begin to feel pressure to succeed.

Usually, when the pressure is relieved, the gymnast becomes relaxed again and can continue to progress rather than regress. When the gymnast is overwhelmed, the most common sign is difficulty with one particular skill or series, such as a flight series on beam. If it continues too long, the athlete begins to lose interest in the sport...not fun anymore...

Many gymnasts are afraid to perform their flight series for other reasons, such as they just do not have enough experience with them or they are not performing the skills with proper technique.

I would recommend doing a high number of series every day on the floor, low beam, and high beam, unless there are injuries or chronic pain. The more series she does, the more comfortable she will feel with it.

Your daughter also needs to perform the series with the correct technique.

I am more than happy to evaluate her series on video and or in person if you think it may be due to improper, or even slightly improper, technique.

Carmela Asks
Subject: 'Balk

Question: My daughter Sarah is 12 years old and is competing in the Ontario Gymnastics Federation Provincial Level 2. Sarah has always placed in the top 3 of her category. In November 2000, Sarah was getting ready to do her tumbling line on her floor routine and she all of a sudden froze. Sarah said she didn't know why this happened and that her brain told her to stop. Sarah stopped doing anything backwards. So, she lost her back handsprings on floor, back handsprings on beam, and fly-a-way on bars. Her coaches said that she 'balked' and it happens a lot to athletes. It has now been over 4 months and slowly Sarah is trying to get all her skills back. Unfortunately, this 'balking' cost her a spot on the Provincial Team this year.
1) What causes a gymnast to 'balk'?
2) What can Sarah do as a gymnast to over come this?
3) What can we do as Parents to support her?
4) What can her Coaches do to help?
I would appreciate your advice and I thank you for taking the time to help.

Hello Carmela,

Your daughter just needs more experience in the sport. Her coaches should be extremely patient with her right now.

Parents should not discuss technique or fears with athletes. Parents should never place any pressure on the athlete regarding skills or scores.

Sometimes when a gymnast is working on too many new skills simultaneously, she becomes overwhelmed and has great difficulty performing. This will hopefully pass when the pressure is reduced.

The most important thing to keep in mind is that she should relax during meets. She should also visualize herself doing her routines perfectly over and over again and eventually she may feel better and score higher.

Carrie Asks
Subject: Things I can do to improve my meet performance.
Question: Whenever I'm at my gym, my routines are great, and I'm not nervous at all. However as soon as I get to meets I'm nervous, and it makes my routines look sloppy. Also, for floor, my music is fast, and I'm sooooo tired at the end. My tumbling lacks as a result. This is my first year level 8 and I really need to get more agility. What are some exercises I could do to improve that? If you could get back to me ASAP I'd appreciate it. Thanx!

Hello Carrie,

The things you mention are actually the responsibility of your coaches or the person who designed your training program.

We had the athletes train in conditions as similar to the meet conditions as possible. We also trained seriously all year round, never sitting in the gym, always very diligent workouts.

If your music is too fast now it is because you just need more time to get used to the routine, again, more routines. You can also try doing back to back routines for endurance or running after the routine.

The things you mention are common for new level 8 athletes. You really need to just follow the coaches and never waste any of your time in the gym.

B Asks
Subject: Motivational Coaching
Question: Hi Karen. Thanks in advance for your time! I am honored!
What sort of repetitive motivational phrases or words of encouragement do you offer your gymnasts?? Is there a phrase unique to gymnastics, like "think 10"...that you want to ingrain in the minds of your gymnasts? I am looking for a short, clever but meaningful phrase to print in a scrapbook for a gymnastics tournament of 6 - 10 year-old girls in Texas. I have been a huge fan all my life but am not familiar with gymnasts' "lingo"...can you help me?
I hope I'm not wasting your time! I admire what you have accomplished! Gymnastics rules at the Olympics for me! Thanks again. B

Hello B

You are not wasting my time at all.
I do not have a short phrase that I repeat to my athletes. I constantly tell them how great they are and remind them they are talented and truly amazing.

My athletes are very excited to come to the gym because they see and feel their progress each month, week, even day.

There was no particular phrase, just enthusiastic coaching. We never wasted time in the gym; although the training is serious, our athletes are very happy.

We encourage smiles and great efforts. Mr. Wang, who was on my staff, used to say the gymnasts must have "good emotions" during training in order to succeed.
Another great coach said quite often that a gymnast must practice "good gymnastics." He also told the athletes that if they want to be a champion, they must act like a champion.

Michele Asks
Subject: uneven bars
Question: I'm a level 5 gymnast. I'm nervous about making the jump from the low bar to the high bar. I've done it a lot of times but some times I just can't do it at all. I've done it in meets very well but can't seem to confidently get over the fear! HELP!

Hello Michele,

Picture yourself doing the skill perfectly very often. Visualizing helps gymnasts with confidence and performance.

In order to overcome a fear, you just have to do the jump several times to get more comfortable with it.

It would be great if your coach remained very close to you until you are comfortable with this skill.

Aubre Asks
Subject: Skills

Question: Do you have tips for getting your glide kip and a back walkover?
Aubre

Hello Aubre,

Walkovers, both back and front, really involve shoulder position and shoulder flexibility. If an athlete thinks about sticking her arm-pits out to get her shoulders above her hands, the skill is much easier and more technically correct.

For glide kips there are several drills. Strength and timing are the key to glide kips.

If you are a gymnast, just keep following your coach's instructions. The skills will come.

If you are a coach you may be interested in ordering a drills book. There are several drills for bars as well as other events in it.

Lauren G Asks
Subject: Injury
Question: Hi!!! My name is Lauren G. I'm 12 years old. I'm a level 6. I have a couple questions. My first question is... I have a cyst in my elbow. The doctor told me that if I didn't take a break for at least 1-2 weeks I could most likely break my elbow. I'm not sure whether or not I should compete in my state meet. If you have any suggestions please let me know. My second question is I get very nervous before all my meets I don't know how to stop that. I have very consistent routines in practices but at meets I loose it. How can I be more prepared for the meets and not get nervous at

the meets? My coaches say I have 9.0 routines but at meets I score 7.0 to 7.4, not very good scores. If you have any suggestions I would love to hear them. Thank you for all your time.
Lauren G

Hello Lauren,

I strongly recommend that you listen to your doctor! If you take the time necessary now to heal, then you may avoid problems later on.

With that said, maybe you can ask your coach to allow you to do different workouts, mostly drills and conditioning for a few weeks until your doctor allows you to go back completely. That would be a good compromise.

You just need more experience in the sport and at meets. The most important thing to keep in mind is that you should relax during meets and try to think of them as fun. Visualize yourself doing your routines perfectly over and over again and eventually you may feel better and score higher.

Parental Concerns

Randell B Asks
Subject: Overcoming fear of moving to a new level Question:
My daughter, age 7, is very physically gifted for gymnastics
(according to her coaches). She just started taking
gymnastics classes in February 2001 and has already been
asked to join a coach's invitation only group. The problem is
she is afraid of going to a new group because she doesn't
know any of the girls. She has developed a comfort level
with the class she is in even though she is so far ahead of
the other girls in the class. The coach recognizes her
abilities and is constantly teaching her very advanced skills.
How can I encourage her to at least give the more advanced
group a try? I've tried taking her to just watch the other group
but she refuses to even try it. By the way, she loves
gymnastics and is taking classes because she wants to, not
because she has been pushed by her mother and I. Any
suggestions would be greatly appreciated. Thank you!

Hello Randell,

If you have been unsuccessful with your attempts to move
your daughter into a higher level group, you may just have to
wait until you daughter feels ready.
If she refuses to go to watch the other class, maybe the
coach will let you videotape it and your daughter can watch it
in the comfort of her own home. She may like her class
because of her friends. If her main focus is social, then she
is best off remaining where she is. She is still very young
and there is plenty of time for her to decide whether she
wants to compete.

Ruth A Asks
Subject: back handspring
Question: My daughter is 6. She has been taking gymnastics since she has been 4. She only takes them (1) hour per week. She has been working on her back handspring for about 7 months. She gets her body over fine but she bends her arms and hits her head. Is this normal? What can I do to help her at home? I am getting worried she is never going to get this skill.
Ruth

Hello,

I would not suggest doing anything with her at home. Hopefully she is not doing this skill at home.

The gymnastics coaches have the job of training your daughter and they should be respected and allowed to do their job exclusively.

Your daughter's technique just needs to be refined and that should come in time.

Mary Asks
Subject: grips- yes or no
Question: My daughter is 9 and started in a rec. class Sept/00. She has since progressed from this to 6 and then 9 and now 12 hours of training. From the beginning she has not wanted to wear grips on the bars. She has had a few tears but seems to be toughing her hands without too much difficulty. Her coach has now said she should have grips due to her lengthened training and it would be to difficult to try

and start using them at higher levels. What would you have to say about this? Also, a parent of a male gymnast told us to use mitchum
Mary

Hello,

The deodorant is to prevent excessive sweating of the hands because sweaty hands can cause the athlete to slip off the bars. That is not necessary.

Every coach has a different opinion on when their athlete should start wearing grips. My athletes didn't wear them too early on because we were more concerned with their hands being too small for the grips and developing their grip/hand strength first.

Other coaches have their gymnasts wear grips from the first day. You should really listen to the coaches in your club; I am sure they have their reasons for their decisions.

Marlene V Asks
Subject: My daughter
Question: My daughter absolutely LOVES gymnastics. We did mommy & me, then she took class once a week for a year; took a year off to try dance; then another year of gymnastics once a week. She is now in a program for "Gifted & Talented" in her gym meeting twice a week for an hour and a half. She will be 8 in May. She says she wants to compete and if they move her up to the first level (level 4) she will start in September. How do I know if she is REALLY ready and good enough and if my gym is best for her?

Hello,

You will not know if she is really ready for the next step until you give it a try.

Competing in this sport is a very large commitment. It is also a commitment for the family. The most important thing you can do is keep your daughter healthy and happy by giving her the proper foods and adequate rest, along with support and encouragement.

Think about what is important while choosing a gym. What do you want out of the sport? Keep in mind the method and philosophy each gym uses. How do the coaches interact with the children? Are the coaches knowledgeable about children as well as the sport? Are the coaches keeping in mind the children's futures? What type of conditioning program does each club offer?

A good program will do injury prevention exercises, body position drills, flexibility, and strength exercises as well as skills and routines. The ratio of coaches to children is not as important as what goes on during the training. It depends on how organized and experienced the coach is. The length of rotation is not necessarily more important than what is being accomplished during the workout.

There are so many aspects to a good program; the bottom line is really what is important to you and your daughter.

Gwen Asks
Subject: skill and level progression

Question: At my current gym the coaching philosophy is to skill and drill for the current level you are in and only work on new skills for the next level in the summer. We always look great at meets and our team wins first and second place all the time. This seems great for the gym reputation but not so great for the individual girls. Is this a normal way to train? If we don't have every skill perfectly for a level we are not promoted to the next level and must wait for the next summer to even practice the skills we need.

Hello Gwen,

The system you describe only allows two months during the entire year for real learning.

We used to have our athletes' condition, drill, skill, and combine skills for the next level while competing on their current level.

We always scored high at meets because we didn't waste any time in the gym. Of the 16-24 hours per week we trained our athletes; (depending upon their level) we had three to four days for routines and two-three days for new skills to be placed in the routines.

New skills were not placed in the routines until they were performed approx. 1000 times successfully.

In other words, we conditioned and learned year round, which limited injury and kept progress steady.

We never held athletes back and we won a lot of meets. If you run a program with the best interest of each individual athlete in mind, your reputation will be highly respected.

Gaylynn Asks
Subject: Training?
Question: I am trying to come up with the best way to organize workouts in our gym. My question is how much time should be spent on each event and how many events should be covered each day. Our workouts are 3 hours a day, two days a week with an additional 3 hours on Fridays being optional.
Levels 4,5,6,8.
Thank You,
Gaylynn

Hello Gaylynn,

The time length of rotation is not more important than what is being accomplished during the workout.

It is more important to accomplish what the children need rather than use length of time on an event as a goal. Just make sure you do not waste a minute of time.

You would be wise to set up stations on each event so that the gymnasts are constantly in motion, never waiting for their turn.

Make sure you are constantly learning new drills for more ideas on return stations for each event. Keep the focus consistent and narrow on each event.

Just remember to be organized and change events when the athletes are no longer making progress that day on the event.

Abby Asks
Subject: temperature
Question: My daughter attends a gym where the temperature in the gym during a workout reaches 90 degrees. I was wondering what the correct temperature for a gym should be. The owner tried to tell me working out in the heat increases stamina. All I can see is exhausted children doing there best to cope. Thanks for you quick reply. Abby
Answer: Many good clubs do not have air conditioning. It is possible that the athletes are getting dehydrated.

Hello Abby,

We always made sure our athletes were very well hydrated, 5 oz Gatorade every 15-20 minutes. After we did a two month study in my club, we learned that Gatorade really does work faster and more efficiently than water.

I don't think there is a guideline in the gymnastics industry regarding room temperature.

I can just tell you that the better physical condition a person is in, the easier they adapt to their environment and even the best conditioned bodies need fluids.

Parent Asks
Subject: Coaching by intimidation and belittling.
Question: I have a gymnast who I think the coach knows has a lot of talent. He pushes her and requires more of her in the

gym for instance, everyone do 5 bar routines and she has to do 20. None of her routines are ever good enough and she may have to do 5 more. She sees that everyone else who can't do as much and who is not talented has to do list with no threats of being sent home. Do 10 routines or go home for a week is a constant comment. Only to my child. Do we confront the coach and have a conference or do we let our child give up her dreams and quit because he is pushing too far? We have considered switching teams but no one local. Do we just put up with any behavior the coach has regardless of whether or not we deem it appropriate?
P.S. She was in top 10 for Nationals Level 9.

Hello,

Coaching by intimidation is wrong. I see it as borderline abuse and would report the coach to the state director after a meeting with the coach if the situation does not improve.

Is this coach also the club owner? If not, you should make sure the owner is also present when you confront the coach.

Many gymnasts travel far to train with a good coach; I had one gymnast travel 2 hours in each direction to train with me.

If your daughter loves the sport and you want a more knowledgeable and patient coach, then call the state director to recommend a good club. There is a great article from December 1991 Technique Magazine called "Motivation vs. Intimidation."

Julie W Asks
Subject: certification

Question: My daughter's gym is fairly small--right now they have 6 coaches, 3 adults and 3 teenagers. None of them are certified in any way. They say that since they don't compete, they don't need to be certified. Is this true? I'm especially concerned about the teenagers--they don't seem to know what they are doing. Any insight you could give me would be greatly appreciated.

Hello,

They are correct. If you are so uncomfortable with the situation, look for another club.

Although there is currently no law regarding gymnastics coaching credentials, it would be wise for each club to have all of their coaches take the safety course and become certified. (1990's)

Jackie J Asks
Subject: choosing a gym
Question: My daughter is a level 5 gymnast. She has been with her gym for about 2 years, with only one of those years competing on the team. The coach we felt was helpful in getting her to that level just left the gym so we are considering moving her.

The gym that she is with now is family owned and the only coaches left are family members, whom we love. However I feel that the coach to child ratio is high. They don't have a dance trainer. (don't know how important this is). No booster club.

We went and interviewed with another gym and we feel that their program is more structured. They have a coach for each apparatus with a 45 minute rotation and other features that we like. I don't want to make my decision only on one coach but only what the gym has to offer.

What are some of the things that I should look for in Gym and in a coach? I'm having a hard time because of my loyalty to our present gym. Please help.
Jackie
ps my daughter very much wants to make the change.

Hello Jackie,

I would suggest finding out exactly why your daughter wants to make the change.

After that, think about what is important to you and her…what do you want to get out of the sport?
Of course, structure is necessary in our sport on the competitive level; keep in mind the method and philosophy each gym uses.

How do the coaches interact with the children? Are the coaches knowledgeable about children as well as the sport? Are the coaches keeping in mind the children's futures?

What type of conditioning program does each club offer? A good program will do injury prevention exercises, body position drills, flexibility, and strength exercises as well as skills and routines.

If the lack of a booster club is a main issue, you can be the one to start it. Some changes can be initiated by the parents while others absolutely can not.

The ratio of coaches to children is not as important as what goes on during the training. There are some coaches that can accomplish more with 20 children than their competitors can with three children; it depends on how organized and experienced the coach is. The length of rotation is not necessarily more important than what is being accomplished during the workout. It is more important to accomplish what the children need rather than use length of time on an event as a goal.

There are so many aspects to a good program; the bottom line is really what is important to you and your daughter.

Coaches Education

Marissa Asks
Subject: gymnastics career opportunities
Question: I am a fifth grader who has been involved in gymnastics for 4 years. I am doing a report on careers in the gymnastic industry. If you could help by answering some questions for me. What kind of education and training is required for entry level jobs? What is the average salary range per year? Are there many jobs available and what are the placement opportunities? Any other basic information will be helpful in my report. Thank you.

Hello Marissa,

There is no formal education required in order to be a gymnastics coach; however, many coaches attend clinics, camps, and other training sessions.

Many have taken coaching or gymnastics classes in college while other coaches have knowledge from practical experience. Many were gymnasts before becoming a coach.

It is sometimes helpful to coaches to have college classes in anatomy, physiology, kinesiology, physics, health, nutrition, or fitness, but these are not required by USA Gymnastics.

There are safety certifications and other certifications available through USA Gymnastics.

Salary varies greatly, depending upon experience and location. And if a good coach is willing to travel or relocate, there are definitely jobs available right now. You may want to look at the classified ads on www.usa-gymnastics.org or www.gymcoach.net to see what club owners are writing in their ads while looking for coaches.

Meghan Asks
Subject: gymnastics
Question: Hi Karen! I am going to be coaching competitive gymnasts from levels 5-8 (but they are YMCA and not as advanced as club 5-8's).
I have never coached gymnastics before but I was a level 9/10 gymnast.
I am very nervous b/c I quit some years ago. If you have any tips for me at all I would really appreciate it! You seem more than qualified!
Thanks!
Meghan

Hello Meghan

First go to www.usa-gymnastics.org and order the compulsory book. It will give you requirements up through level 7. You may also want to order the code of points eventually.

Go to as many clinics and meetings that USA Gymnastics organizes. Call the local clubs or even the one you trained at to see if there are any upcoming events you can attend. National Congress is in Cleveland, Ohio this year and all that information will be in the USAG site. If you can get there, do it!

Another great learning tool is attending camps as a guest coach so that you can watch the more experienced coaches.

Eventually you may want to be a regular coach at a camp. Camps are a wonderful way to meet other coaches and share ideas.

You may also want to order my book of drills which was originally written for a group of YMCA coaches in Massachusetts. The drills are perfect for the developing gymnasts. We used the drills with our level 1-10 gymnasts. www.gymcoach.sport.new.net

Ashley Asks
Subject: level 7 gymnastics
Question: I need to know if you can tell me the skill requirements for USAG level 7 optional. If at all possible I need all apparatus requirements.
Thank you

Hello Ashley,

I have not coached level 7 in a long time. I have coached level 8 and up for many years, mostly level 9's.

You may want to try the USA Gymnastics site, www.usa-gymnastics.org to see if the information is there and order the USAG Compulsory Book as well as the FIG Code of Points.

Becky H Asks
Subject: Bars- the counterswing
Question: Karen,
Unfortunately, I am the local gym and fairly new at coaching which means I still need help with my question. The counterswing, fly-back, is often used as a release skill for

high school gymnastics. That is what I coach and I also coach a small club team. Although our skills are different than USAG, we still produce quality gymnastics in the state I am in. I would really appreciate any references to materials I could gather to find out how to help my athletes perform this skill.

Do you have any suggestions for lead up drills for teaching the counterswing on bars, and, what suggestions do you have to help gymnasts eliminate that nasty tap on counterswings. (I know generally it means they are releasing too early, but what other tips can you offer?)
Becky

Hello Becky,

The best thing for you to do at this point is to go to a good gymnastics club several times to observe how they work with their young athletes on bars.

I still strongly recommend you spend time in a reputable club with very experienced coaches and attend several coaching clinics. You will have to travel, but that is the only way.

It is not safe or advised for you or anyone to coach from a book.

USA Gymnastics does have a web-site and they have sold books in the past, but once again, it is more wise to spend the time and energy traveling to higher level coaches.

Peter P Asks
Subject: coaching ratio

Question: What ratio of PE instructor to number of children is recommended in a general gymnastics gym course for children from 7 to 12 years of age with no previous experience in gymnastics?
Should physical education instructors have any special training to teach general gymnastics to young children?

Hello Peter,

In a private gymnastics club the ratio is most often under 10 children per instructor. In schools the ratio of children to teachers seems to be higher.

Most physical education teachers take a course in gymnastics as part of their physical education degree. I personally feel there should be more training because teaching and spotting are skills that must be practiced in addition to being able to analyze the skills being performed by the athletes.

Injuries or Pain

Kelley V Asks
Subject: Back Pain during Walkovers
Question: My daughter is a Level 6 gymnast. We just had a CT Scan of her spine because the doctor thought she had a stress fracture. Fortunately, that was not the case. Unfortunately, we do not know where her pain is coming from. The doctor feels it must be in her muscles or ligaments or both. She was given a few stretches to do from an athletic trainer. Those help some, but the pain is there to some extent.

What can she do about her back pain during back walkovers on the beam? This mainly occurs during back walkovers on the beam, and then after practice her back is sore. Sometimes it is sore for days. This can be a real problem during meets.

Her doctor has said to only do the back walkovers when she is pain free. And then to only do a few at a time.

Her coaches don't notice any bad form. Can you tell us what could possibly cause her muscles or ligaments to cause such pain? Are there any exercises you can recommend? Is there anything we can do?
Kelly

Hello Kelly,

I am sorry to hear of your daughter's back pain.

Sometimes when a gymnast's shoulders are lacking flexibility she is forced to involve her lower back to perform certain skills, including walkovers. I would check this first.

Another important thing to look at is the technique of the walkover and most of her other skills. The walkovers should really involve more shoulders therefore causing less stress on the back.

It is extremely important to make every effort to perfect basic skills for safety, technique, and longevity in the sport.

A visit to a physical therapist may be a great idea if her shoulders are already very flexible and her walkovers are being done through her shoulders.

It is so great that you are on top of the situation because after her gymnastics career she will need her back for the rest of her life.

You are welcome to email me again regarding this situation or others.

Kathy Asks
Subject: Shin splints
Question: What causes shin splints? How should this condition be treated? How can it be prevented?

Hello Kathy,

I have heard several theories from sports experts on shin splints. The one that seems logical, although I am not sure if it is scientifically correct, is that the pain is caused when the nerve located in the arch of the foot which runs up the front of your leg strikes the floor repeatedly, causing pain and inflammation.

I do know that …
Ice helps the pain and inflammation.

And that good, shock absorbing arches along with heel cushions in your shoes all of the time, helps prevent further pain.

The following was the treatment my athletes have followed for many years and it has worked well.

1) They placed heel cushions and soft arch supports in their gymnastics shoes for all vault, tumbling, and dance training.
2) They also placed heel cushions with arch supports in their everyday shoes and sneakers.
3) My athletes competed with these cushions in their gymnastics shoes on vault and occasionally floor exercise. Bars and beam were done barefoot most of the time.
4) They iced when in pain, mostly after each workout.
5) Much of their tumbling and vault training was moved to the trampoline. The amount of running, jumping, and tumbling we allowed on the regular floor exercise mats was reduced drastically.

We noticed that those gymnasts with shin splints adjusted their training, but had the same result\skill after a 6 month period.

We eventually changed our training program to prevent shin splints by reducing the amount of jumps per work out and moving a great deal of the tumbling and jumps to the trampoline.

The athletes muscles were trained the same as with the impact, but without the pain!

Ashli Asks
Subject: fulls and conditioning?
Question: HI!
Okay I used to be really good at twisting everything like that but I had screws put in my ankles (fractured it too many times) and now every time I go to do my full I only pull a half or maybe I can get 3/4.... I can never get my fulls around. I don't really think its because of my ankles but I was just wondering if you knew any drills or anything I could do to get my full all the way around. I pull left if you needed to know that. Also I was wondering if you knew any good exercises for my ankles to make them stronger now. Thanks a ton!!
Ash

Hello Ashli,

Sorry to hear about your ankles...ouch!
Here are two ankle exercises from my drills book...

Towel Exercises
1. Stand with toes and top portion of feet on a towel or soft cloth.
2. Using your toes, pull towel so that it ends up crunched under feet.

3. As you are pulling towel with feet, your arches usually lift so that you are on the outer edges of your feet.
4. This usually helps align the feet and ankles for more comfortable and safer landings.
5. Once this is mastered, a small weight can be placed on the towel.

Ankle Drills
1. Bend knees to feel a stretch in the achilles and ankles.
2. Keeping knees bent, lift heels as high as possible, pushing feet forward.
3. Keeping heels high, straighten knees, to a releve position.
4. Lower heels to start again.

Your twisting...
1. Make sure your round-off back handspring is quick, tight, and efficient.
2. And make sure your layout is tight and high.

According to Bela, when I asked him his opinion on twisting about 10 years ago, he said that arm position is not as important as making one side of your body shorter than the other side.

That has worked for many of my gymnasts too! In other words, contract your muscles in the front side of your body (obliques) when you pull your arms down to twist. Make sure your eyes follow your hands.

Teresa Asks
Subject: injuries

Question: My 13 year old daughter is training level 8. She is 4ft 9in tall and weighs 76 lbs. She has had 4 broken bones (wrist, two great toes and 5th metatarsal) in the last year. All were from gymnastics incidences. She is getting a cast off of her right foot today from a badly sprained ankle about 3 weeks ago. The orthopedic doctor says she has just had a run of "bad luck". She was evaluated by a Pedi Endocrinologist who says she is small but normal. Her coach says she gets hurt because she is "sloppy and loose". She has NO desire to quit gym. Am I crazy to let her keep going???? She trains 30 hrs/wk during the summer and 22 hrs/wk during school year. An "outsiders" opinion would be so greatly appreciated!!

Hello Theresa,

It sounds like you should inquire about the coaches' qualifications and knowledge. You might want to call the USAG State Chairman and request a list of the best clubs in the area.

A good coaching friend of mine once said that gymnasts are similar to pure breed race horses. Because they are expected to perform above and beyond the average, they need to be fed a diet above and beyond the average. We were discussing how so many of our gymnasts do not eat well enough.

To me it sounds like your daughter has not had enough calcium or enough of the proper conditioning, such as with weights in order to build bone density.

She may also need to get more flexible in her ankles and other areas.

Try looking for a physical therapist that also carries a "CSCS" certification. That is a certified strength and conditioning specialist. It is their job to bring the athlete through the healing and then from the normal\healed to the above normal in condition.

You may also want to speak with a sports nutritionist.

Cheryl W Asks
Subject: Elbow injury
Question: At the beginning of this past December I sprained 3 ligaments in my right elbow. I followed doctor's orders and stayed off of it for 6 weeks. However, at the beginning of February when I started tumbling again, I wasn't doing very good at all and people said that they could tell by the way I was tumbling which arm I had hurt. I was just wondering if you had any suggestions on how I can stop "favoring" that arm, and maybe some strengthening exercises for it. I went to about 3 or 4 classes but was doing so bad that it frustrated me and I decided to take a break. I am eager to get back in it, but I don't want to keep tumbling the way I was. Any thoughts would be greatly appreciated - sorry this is so long.
Thank you!!
Cheryl :)

Hello Cheryl,

You should really see a physical therapist or someone with a CSCS Certification. For safety reasons, you need to get back into the sport slowly.

After several weeks your muscles have most likely atrophied causing you to lose strength. The coaches should be giving you specialized conditioning as well.
Many variations of push ups, including handstand pushups, and plyometrics for your upper body, such as handstand hops, as well as your lower body would be helpful.

You are welcome to contact me again.

Kim Asks
Subject: advice
Question: My daughter is 13 and completed two seasons at level 8. Her highest score was a 35.75. She is best on vault and then followed by bars. She started having knee problems this year. The kneecap was jumping out of place and then came down wrong on a full on the floor and had a growth plate injury to the knee. We have had problems with the owners of the gym as a result of the booster club at the present time and she is not training. We would like to know your gut feeling about her future in the sport with the injuries. (The knee still gives her trouble, even after therapy.) We would also like to get your idea on the best number of training hours for a training level 9. Do you also know cost averages for that number of hours. There is one other gym in the area, but the cost is much more. Thanks for your advice.

Hello Kim,

The best thing to do is find a great physical therapist and a certified strength and conditioning coach to deal with her injuries and get a good basic conditioning program.

Try calling the USAG State Chairman and ask for a list of the best clubs in your area. Every club is different regarding number of hours. My level nines and tens trained 24 hours per week and not a minute was wasted. We had a serious training program and very few injuries.

I can not tell you what your daughters' future holds. Maybe the best thing to do is ask her what she wants to do and then figure out a way for her to do that. Many gymnasts travel a great deal in order to get the proper training.

Amanda H Asks
Subject: injuries
Question: Hello!
I'm wanting to know a little information about a torn rotator cuff. How would you help to rehabilitate one of your gymnasts after surgery? What form of condition would you seek for the gymnast? I'm doing a research, for a class. I would truly appreciate your response. Thank you
Sincerely,
Amanda H

Hello Amanda,

The first thing I have done in the past has been to consult with the doctor that performed the surgery, the physical therapist, and my sports scientist.

I have always requested prescriptions, a list of "do's and don'ts" from all three prior to any actions.

Most of the time they suggested the popular windshield wiper exercise...lie on side, elbows at ribs against body, bent at 90 degrees, then bring knuckles toward ceiling as if both lower arms are acting as windshield wipers...using extremely light weight.

Another popular exercise is simple, small arm circles, again with extremely light weights, never more than 1 1/2 pound dumb bells.

You may want to ask a few Physical Therapists and go the web-site for the National Academy of Sports Medicine to find some articles.

Remember to give full credit to those who supply information in your paper.

Lauren G Asks
Subject: Injury
Question: Hi!!! My name is Lauren G. I'm 12 years old. I'm a level 6. I have a couple questions.
I have a cyst in my elbow. The doctor told me that if I didn't take a break for at least 1-2 weeks I could most likely break my elbow. I'm not sure whether or not I should compete in my state meet. If you have any suggestions please let me know.
I get very nervous before all my meets I don't know how to stop that. I have very consistent routines in practices but at meets I loose it. How can I be more prepared for the meets and not get nervous at the meets? My coaches say I have

9.0 routines but at meets I score 7.0 to 7.4, not very goods scores. If you have any suggestions I would love to hear them. Thank you for all your time.
Lauren G

Hello Lauren,

I strongly recommend that you listen to your doctor! If you take the time necessary now to heal, then you may avoid problems later on.

Maybe you can ask your coach to allow you to do drills and conditioning until your doctor allows you to go back completely.

You just need more experience at meets. Keep in mind you should relax during meets and try to have fun. Visualize yourself doing your routines perfectly over and over again.

Physical Preparation or Training

Melissa Asks
Subject: Training for college gymnastics
Question: I used to be a level 6 gymnast but I didn't get to compete level 6 before I moved a long way away from my gym. Would I have to compete level 6 if I went back to gymnastics? I am also training Level 8 tumbling and vaulting and I want to try for college gymnastics but I don't know how I would train since I only want to compete floor and vault. Do you know what kind of level of skills that you need to have to go and compete in college?

Hello,

Yes, you would most likely have to continue level 6, unless you qualified to level 7. Gymnasts can no longer skip level 7.

I am not sure on the college rules, but I have noticed that usually in order to compete in college you should be a level 10 by your senior year and be competing successfully with consistently high all around scores.

You should go to the NCAA web-site for their rules and you can go to the USA Gymnastics web-site www.usa-gymnastics.org for more information as well.

Laura Asks
Subject: summer training camps
Question: I would like to send my daughters to a quality summer gymnastics training camp near or in Michigan. My daughters are age 11 & level 8, and age 8 and training as a level 7. We would like this to be a day camp. We live near

Flint, Michigan. We would like a camp that offers a small gymnast to trainer ratio.

Hello Laura,

The best camp that I know of is USAGTC held in Mt Holyoke, MA. www.usgymnasticscamps.com

Other great camps are Karolyi's in Texas and International Gymnastics in Pennsylvania.

The governing body also has a web-site where you may find some information: www.usa-gymnastics.org

Ingrid D Asks
Subject: A slow gymnast
Question: Hello Karen,
My name is Ingrid D and I'm a gymnastic coach for over 7 years. I'm from the Netherlands.
I've got a question about one of my gymnasts. She now 14 and about 1.60 meter. She has a good figure and has good talent for gymnastics (strength and flexibility). Only everything she does, looks so slow and heavy, especially on the uneven bars and tumbling.
How can I train this, so it improves and she becomes quicker in her movements.
I'm sorry if my English is not correct.
Kind regards,
Ingrid

Hello Ingrid,

I have seen many coaches try to increase their athlete's strength and really have good intentions, but they end up slowing down their athletes because they are only training the athlete's strength not their speed or power.

You need to condition your athlete for your sport try to simulate the movements of the sport through conditioning.

You can increase your athletes running speed by having her run downhill to have her muscles become accustomed to reacting quicker rather than having your athlete pull things while trying to run, which may actually slow her down.
The fact that an athlete is pulling something while attempting to run is actually not training running speed.

Another mistake I have seen is when the coach has their athletes doing tons of pushups which do increase strength, but do not simulate gymnastics skills like handstand shrugs and hops. Shrugs and hops get the athlete stronger and train shoulder speed and position. The shrugs help the stretched shoulder position on bars, and the hops help the block/push/rebound during tumbling.

So do more conditioning to fit the sport. Train drills, body positions, plyometrics, and muscle endurance rather than only general strength exercises.

My drills book has several drills for bars, running, dance elements, and press handstands.

You can go to: www.gymcoach.sport.new.net for more information.

Diane N Asks
Subject:
Question: Hi Karen,
What criteria, physiological and psychological, do coaches look for when deciding whether a child is capable of becoming an elite gymnast (female). Also, what is an optimal age to "go elite" at? It seems to really be successful (i.e. compete internationally and be on the National Team) that one must become elite at 11 or 12.

Finally, do you consider plyometrics a useful training method to help develop quickness and power for tumbling and vaulting?

Thank you,
Diane

Hi Diane,

I looked more for the fire in the child's eyes when deciding whether or not I would accept a child on the team. We had a very serious training program.
I also watched how diligent the athlete was during training, their time management, stress management, eating and sleeping habits, and the amount of support from their family.

Of course strength and flexibility are extremely important. The optimal age is when the athlete is physically and psychologically ready. Each athlete is an individual.

Yes! Plyometric Training is necessary in our sport, but only with a knowledgeable coach and one time per week because it can be stressful on the joints. Over training can cause chronic aches and pains and literally destroy an athlete's competitive career.

Cheryl R Asks
Subject: Level 6
Question: Our daughter belongs to a YMCA gymnastics team that does not currently have a Level 6 coach. Therefore, all gymnasts that have mandated out of Level 5 must perform Level 7 next year. The coaches feel that the variances between the two levels are not that great and that the scoring will be easier at this level. As the parent of a 9 year old, I'm concerned that she will be missing necessary tricks and may need to develop more before going into the optional level. If we do transfer her to a private gym within the next few years I'm sure she will require the Level 6 scores. What is your feeling on skipping this Level?

Hello,

You are right. USA Gymnastics is stricter with level mobility than YMCA's are. I have been involved with both.

Most often USAG clubs will require her to register level 5 to start if she has never gone to a USAG meet. If you are planning to make the move to a private club, do it sooner rather than later.

I have seen level 10 YMCA gymnasts have to learn and compete levels 5, 6, and 7 in order to compete on the higher levels in USAG.

One gymnast is now elite in both USAG and YMCA, but she was forced to go through the correct qualification requirements to get to her level.

I did however petition a gymnast into level 6 one year who came to me from a YMCA. She qualified to level 8 in her first two meets that season and was a level 9 within a year. Every club and every state is different.

Sweetia Asks

Subject: Conditioning
Question: Hi Karen!
I'm a level 7 gymnast and I would like to start conditioning at home. I don't think I'm strong enough. Also I have horrible eating habits. I'm a vegetarian. So, could you help me put together Conditioning and Eating Plans?
Thanx soooooo much,
Sweetia

Hello Sweetia,

I do not recommend conditioning or anything at home. The rest in between workouts is just as important as the workouts themselves. Your muscles need time to heal.

As far as eating, try to eat a wide variety of foods. I never enjoyed meat as a child or teen, so for many years, I followed a diet similar to a vegetarian's. Beans, milk, yogurt, cheese, peanuts...all have protein in them and can at times be substituted for meats if necessary.

Also make sure you are getting plenty of carbohydrates such as rice, pasta, and bread. And, of course, eat plenty of fruits and vegetables. Make sure you are starting your day off right with a good breakfast too.

It may be wise for you to purchase a small nutrition book and learn about the content of foods then come up with a menu that you enjoy.

During workouts, it may be a good idea for you to start drinking Gatorade in order to give your muscles what they need when they need it.

Clare Asks
Subject: I have trouble doing splits
Question: Hi~ I have trouble with doing splits; I mean I can't really do them. Can you help??

Hello,

Here are a few of the exercises for flexibility.

*Please keep in mind that you could get injured if you do not do these exercises carefully and correctly. You should have a qualified coach supervise your training.

Hip Flexor Stretch

1. Lie on back on horse or spotting block or mat stack.
2. Make sure your buttocks is at edge.
3. Hold one knee close to chest, bent leg.
4. Lift other leg above body with toes pointed toward ceiling.

5. Slowly lower relaxed leg so that it is hanging below the level of the horse.
6. Make sure the hanging leg is lined up with the hip and not off to the side.
7. The hip flexor will be slowly stretched while hanging in this position.
8. Gymnast may wear a light ankle weight, depending upon level.

Hip Flexor/Hamstring Stretch

1. Kneel on floor with one leg in front of body.
2. Shift weight to front leg, pushing hips forward.
3. Once hips are forward, lift back foot, bending at knee.
4. Make sure foot is not over the knee for the safest and most efficient stretch.
5. Keeping feet in place, shift the hips back to stretch the front leg's hamstring muscles.
6. Make sure gymnast is not sitting on back foot and that the very tops of the thighs are touching to keep the stretch square. Stretching square will help keep the splits and leaps square.

Partner Standing Stretch & Strength

1. Allow experienced partner to stretch leg by lifting high enough to feel stretch in back of legs, mostly hamstrings.
2. Make sure to keep supporting leg straight and hips even. Keep supporting foot flat on floor and both legs turned out slightly.
3. Partner is doing the lifting/stretching for gymnast for the first 10-15 seconds.

4. Once the partner is done stretching gymnast, have the gymnast resist the partner for another 10-15 seconds as partner continues to stretch gymnast slowly and carefully.
5. After the resistance portion of the exercise, have the partner hold the heel of the gymnast slightly lower than the highest stretching point and then allow the gymnast to lift her leg up and out of partner's hand several times quickly.

Once the gymnast is able to lift her leg higher, have her lift and hold for as long as possible, often only a few seconds.

David L Asks
Subject: Strength in Female gymnasts
Question: Hi Karen
I have two daughters ages 12.5 & 14 who are involved in Trampoline & Tumbling They are both Level 10. Both have participated in USA Gymnastics Trampoline & Tumbling Finals three years in a row.
Can you direct me to some resources to learn how to build strength in these girls without significant increased hypertrophy?
I read of one technique of weight training that uses maximum weight, with minimal reps and intermediate rest intervals
I think it is called: Brief Maximum Effort or Repeated Maximum Effort.
I want maximum strength from minimum size. I want to reduce their strength deficit.
Any help is appreciated.
Thank you

Hello,

It is the job of the coach to design the strength-training program as part of the sport-specific training.

Additional training outside the coaches training could actually interfere with and negatively affect the training sessions with their coach.

I strongly suggest you speak with the coach and if you feel the coach is inadequate, please find one you and your children respect.

Denyse Asks
Subject: Young gymnast
Question: My daughter just turned 5 in March and has been doing gymnastics for about 1 1/2 years. She just got invited to team but her coaches are wondering what to do with her. She cannot compete for 2 years but has been doing the level 5 routines on all events since January. Her coaches did not want to keep her with the pre-team training program because she clearly needs the challenge. (she is highly competitive with her group of girls) She gets bored very easily and picks up skills very easily. They do not want her to compete with the GI JO program at our club and say she cannot compete Level 4 until she is 6 which will not be until March, 2003, so they are kind of boggled as to how to handle her without her getting too bored. I think what they are trying to tell me is that they do not want any feelings hurt because she will not get very much attention since she will not be competing and yet they would still like to have her work with the L5 girls, but then what if she gets bored. I really do not know, but they have had a couple of

discussions with me before they even invited her to team this last month. What do you suggest?

Hello,

The coaches should know what to do with a young talented gymnast.

I had the same situation with a gymnast of mine. I trained her for a few years before she was old enough to compete. Each time she was more than capable of competing the next level, we had to wait until she was old enough.

We just trained her consistently and made competitions second in priority. She was one of only 5 gymnasts at age seven competing in the USA at one time, was on the first National TOPS Team, became a NY State Champion (USAG) on bars at level 8, and then a Level 10 National Champion (YMCA) on bars. She has since retired after a wonderful gymnastics career.

The USAG Level 1-10 and Elite competitions are not the only avenues to take a young gymnast. They should be getting her strong, flexible and training bigger skills now.

She is the right age for the TOPS Program too. I do not agree that a parent should be making training decisions, but the coaches should already be aware of and capable of this program and training.

Two useful sites for you and the coaches:
For TOPS information: www.usa-gymnastics.org

For conditioning and drills specifically designed for developmental gymnasts.

Catrina Asks
Subject: Beginning Gymnastics
Question: I am a 15 year old girl and I Would like to participate in the sports of gymnastics. I know most people start when they are younger. Do you think I will have a chance at excelling in the sport?

Hello Catrina,

There is no age limit or anything of the sort when it comes to starting gymnastics. I have seen adults enter the sport and reach very respectable levels. Hard work and determination will decide how far you go!

Chin HV Asks
Subject: PLEASE HELP...!!
Question:
Hello: I would like to involve and joint the Gymnastics world when I watch the Olympic Games. But I am now becoming older, 25 years old. I have not involved any exercises before that. Is it possible for me for start to learn and joint it. I also got other problems of my body structure where I have just been found few months ago when I was 25 years old (I did not realize all those problems before that -- since 24 years --). I found that I got the bow legs; the right leg is bower than the left one. I got over pronation on my knee and angle joint especially on my right leg. I also found that the bower right leg is about 7 mm longer than the left leg. I also got the uneven (unbalance) shoulder where my right shoulder is lower. I am thin and under weight, 167cm, 47kg.

When I found these problems, I felt really disappointed and upset. Will they block and destroy my hope and ambition? Before that, I found that a lot of people got a strong and straight leg, muscular and strengthen body. Is it mean that I would worse than them? Can you give me any suggestion and guidance? Is it possible for me to involve into the gymnastic world and reach the competition level?
 Chin HV

Hello,

I know that many gymnastics centers have adult gymnastics classes for beginners and for former gymnasts.

You should look in the telephone book or go to one of the yellow page websites and type in gymnastics instruction. Once you have found some telephone numbers call the ones near you and ask if they have any classes available.

Many people enter the sport as adults in order to gain strength and flexibility. Many others join just to make friends and have fun.

J Asks
Subject: Levels
Question: How is it decided which women gymnasts compete at Regional & National meets at the Junior Olympic level? How do they qualify? Also, how does a gymnast become an elite and qualify to the national championships? I'm just starting to learn about this sport :)

Hello J,

Usually the scores from state meets decide who goes to Regionals and the top places are the ones that often compete in the east/west meet.

I do not remember the rules to become an elite but I do know they are tested and are required to perform certain skills.

You may find some helpful information on the www.usa-gymnastics.org site.

Janice Y Asks
Subject: Loss of abdominal ripples (muscle tone)
Question: Last November my daughter moved from one club to another as her home club owner had to shut it doors for personal reasons. The club we are with now has done a lot for her in terms of skills, especially floor, but there is definitely not as much time spent on flexibility, cardio and muscle building/toning/maintaining. As a parent I am reluctant to push these points as our head coach feels that as I am not a coach, I don't really know much about the day to day intricacies of a four hour training session. My daughter has been involved in competitive gymnastics for about three years - one year at the compulsory level and two at the optional level. I have spent almost every hour watching her train that she has been in the gym so I am aware of more than most parents. Plus, I used to be heavily involved in sports myself (basketball, volleyball and figure skating) so I am well versed in how important basics are to any sport.
Last summer Jessica had those wonderful ripples in the abdomen that let us know how hard she had worked at her conditioning and weight training. All of that is now gone and

all she has is a stomach with skin (even a little pouch that shows how things are not as tight).
What can I do, as a parent, to make the coach realize that something is not working as well, or is being left out, or is lacking, etc, without making her feel like I am stepping on her toes and being totally critical of her training sessions. I read in your bio that you have a book of conditioning and drills. Is it for sale and, if so, how much is it and where can I get it? I live in Newfoundland, Canada, so please bear that in mind. Anything you have to offer me on anything I have said would be greatly appreciated. Thank you for your time and I look forward to hearing from you.

Hello Janice,

I am sorry to hear you are not completely satisfied with your daughter's training. If you are so unhappy it may be wise to find another club. You did mention that the current coach has done a lot for your daughter though. Is your daughter happy and in a safe program? Those should be among your top priorities.

I agree that proper conditioning is extremely important, that is why I wrote the book, which was originally done for a team of coaches I worked with.
When I was a club owner I did not allow a parent to influence my coaching. I was the coach and they were the parents. Most parents did not have a clue about designing or running a training program.

Gymnastics is very different from other sports and only those involved on the competitive level for a very long time should be doing this job, not people from other sports.

Changes in young girl's bodies happen all the time, they are constantly growing and changing their eating habits as well as their activity levels.

Yes, I did write a drills book and it can be ordered online if you go to my web-site.

Physical Requirements

Brandi Asks
Subject: back handsprings
Question: I am 5 foot 7 inches and 125 lbs. I want to do a back handspring and have limited if any tumbling experience. I want to be able to do the back handspring by fall try-outs but my mom doesn't know anyone that can help and doesn't have any extra money to get me into tumbling classes. Can you tell me the steps so that she can help me learn how.
Also, She thinks that I am too big (in height) to do any tumbling but I think that she is wrong. Is this true? If you can't tell me the exact steps, is there any way that you can give me tips on the stunt? Thank you very much for your help on the subject.

Hello,

I will not teach you a skill through email. It is not safe.

You are definitely not too tall! Does your school have a gymnastics team/club? Or maybe the local YMCA or dance studio has a basic tumbling/acrobatics class. They are usually less expensive that a private gymnastics club.

History and Research

Sports psychology
Question: hi,
I am doing a paper on how the mind and thinking (psychology) affects gymnastics/the gymnast. What are some ways that it affects it and where can I go to find information on this subject? All and any help will be greatly appreciated.
thanks a billion
Alexis

Hello Alexis,

I do not do homework questions, but I am happy to give you direction for information.

You need to go the library and get sports psychology books.

One great source for sports psychology is Dr. Joe Massimo. He wrote some articles and books about gymnasts. Look up his name in the library.

Another great source is the magazine called Technique Magazine, by USA Gymnastics. It seems there is a mental article in each issue. The main office for USA Gymnastics is in Indianapolis. They also sell books and other learning materials so you may want to ask for a catalog if possible. The web address is www.USA-Gymnastics.org.

Judy Asks
Subject: elite gymnastics

Question: Where do I find information regarding "elite" level gymnastics? I have a niece who'll be competing at this level and I'm trying to understand the qualifications to become an elite as well as the number of athletes involved. I'm having difficulty understanding what elite means with regard to the "national" team or "international" team or no team? Also, she's in the process of changing gyms because hers is in the process of losing the staff and potentially being sold. What should her parents be most concerned about when selecting this new gym?

Hello,

Congratulations to your niece!

When selecting a gym, her parents should keep in mind the experience of the coaches.

They can call the governing office and ask for the state director's contact information. The state director can usually recommend a gym.

You can also find information on the following site: www.usa-gymnastics.org.

Hayley K Asks
Subject: intensive training
Question: I am writing a dissertation on the social effects of intensive gymnastics training on young gymnasts.
Hayley K

Hello Hayley,

I do not do homework questions, but I am happy to give you direction.

You need to go the library and get sports psychology books. One great source for sports psychology is Dr. Joe Massimo. He wrote some articles and books about gymnasts. Look up his name in the library.

Another great source is the magazine called Technique Magazine, by USA Gymnastics. It seems there are articles regarding mental training in most of the issues.

Try to get a copy of the USA Gymnastics Magazine Jan/Feb 1993 issue for the article, "Gymnastics, Who Wants To Be Normal." by Jim Roe, Virginia International Gymnastics Schools.

The main office for USA Gymnastics is in Indianapolis. They also sell books and other learning materials so you may want to ask for a catalog if possible. The web address is www.usa-gymnastics.org.

P. D. Asks
Subject: Been getting the run around
Question: Do you use trampolines in your training facility?
If so, where do you get replacement springs?

Hello,

I no longer have a club. But, yes we had two flatbed trampolines, a double mini trampoline, and a mini trampoline. They were extremely useful in training for body awareness, strength, endurance, dance, tumbling, vaulting, injury prevention, injury rehabilitation, and fun!

Replacement springs can be purchased from equipment companies. Type the words "gymnastics equipment" in any search engine.

You can also go to www.usa-gymnastics.org and click on Industry Members. There should be an equipment company on that site.

Mrs. S. Asks
Subject: history of gymnastics
Question: Hello we are MID SUFFOLK GYM CLUB and we are doing a carnival float and the theme is the past 50 years. We thought that we would do it on the Olympics and who had one gold silver and bronze for the over all competition winners. We have only been able to find the results for the last two competitions, would you know where to find any more.

Thank you

Hello,

Try doing the research as if you are researching anything else. Go to the library and read through the books and go to the internet and type in keywords such as "Olympics" or "gymnastics" or even "history of gymnastics."

Good luck with your project!

Katie Asks
Subject: Help!
Question: I am writing a paper in my English Comp. class about the differences between Gymnastics and Power Tumbling. I belonged to a Tumbling Team for 10 years, and competed up to level 10, so I know a lot about Tumbling, but not so much about Gymnastics. I basically just need to know about the different organizations (USAGYMNASTICS, etc.), the levels, and about the competitions. If you know of a good site that I could go to for this info. I would greatly appreciate it.
Thank you. Katie

Hello,

www.usa-gymnastics.org,
www.gymcoach.sport.new.net,
www.ncaa.org,
www.usgymnasticscamps.com,
www.humankinetics.com,
www.intlgymnast.com,
www.youthsport.net

Alicia Asks
Subject: rings skill
Question: why is the skill "skin the cat" called that?

Hello Alicia,

Good question! I really don't have that answer. Try posting it on the message board and see if anyone else knows.

Opening or Setting Up a Club

Tammy Asks
Subject: Rec Op/ Starting Comp Teams
Question: I would like to start a competitive team program out at the Air Force base where I have my own program. How do I start? I have coached up thru level 6 but just can't seem to figure out how to start up a team. Do you know the code of points for Rec OP?

Hello Tammy,

I am doing the same thing for a local YMCA right now. The following list comes from the plan I wrote up today in order to get their team program started. I deleted a few that would not be useful to any program other than this particular YMCA.

1. You need to get the kids strong, flexible, and keep making their basic skills better.
2. Get USAG athlete memberships and then call the other clubs/teams for meet schedules.
3. See if they'll allow you to bring athletes to one of their workouts and workout as one big team for a day...great learning experience! The kids learn that competitors can also be friends.
4. Each summer go to camps, such as USAGTC or IGC and learn how to teach as many skills on the next two levels as possible, that would be levels 7 and 8 for you this year.
5. Speak with at least a dozen experienced coaches to learn new drills and ideas.

It takes time and energy, but it is a great experience to turn a group of individual athletes into a strong team.

Gymnastics Things to Do List:

Welcome letter to athletes: revise, print, mail
Write up guidelines for athletes and parents
Call USA Gymnastics 800-345-4719/317-237-5050 for:
Pro and Club Membership information
TOPS information
Coaches Level 1-4 and 5-7 Training Videos, Compulsory music and Book, FIG Code of Points
Biomechanics book by Gerry George-every gym needs one
www.gymfoundation.org
www.usa-gymnastics.org
Call USAIGC 302-656-3706 for:
Membership information
STEP program information
View videos with staff and athletes
Write press release
Call Mike Jacobsen 561-743-8550 ASAP for:
Camp brochures - USAGTC held at Mt Holyoke
Camp equipment prices
Possible clinic for athletes and coaches
Call equipment companies for brochures used and new equipment.
Fund raising
Online search:
Sponsor companies
Apparel companies
Call apparel companies for brochures
GK 800-345-4087
Write list of necessary equipment

List of necessary apparel and supplies
"Wish List" for gymnastics program
Take pictures and/or video ASAP to use as starting point, press releases, and sponsorship letters.
Write letters to neighborhood companies and corporations including wish list and pictures.

The above list does not include staff training or seminars that are necessary on occasion.

Which base are you on? I am available to do clinics and video evaluations of athletes. You are welcome to contact me via e-mail again.

James W. Jr. Asks
Subject: Safety area beyond tumbling mats
Question: I am looking at installing regulation size tumbling mats at our school for instruction on tumbling and cheerleading. What are the recommended clearances beyond the end and sides of the mats for safety? One of the four walls is mirrored and another wall has 3 stairs that extend the full length of the floor for access to a stage. Any help would be appreciated. References to written standards would also be helpful.
Thank you - Jim in Texas

Hello Jim,

Common sense would be a good judge. Keep safety in mind while setting up your equipment.

I would keep the tumbling at least six feet from walls and much further from the stairs.

As far as rules for set up for gymnastics competition, the "Rules & Policies" book and the "USAG Safety Manual" are used as guides.

Many clubs make great efforts to use these guides for training as well as for competitions.

John Asks
Subject: Starting a Gym
Question: Karen,
This is a tall order, but I am seeking direction in opening a gymnastics center. I have 3 daughters currently in club gymnastics. Two are participating at level 10.
I have commitment from three of the optional coaches, at the current gym, to "come on board" if I were to proceed.
I have a strong management background and performed gymnastics as a youth, but little direct experience in operating a gym. The demographics are favorable and I have some capital and will commit to full-time attention to the business. Karen, can you direct me to where I can find help to start on the right foot?
John

Hello John,

What State are you in? I may be able to give you some telephone numbers including my own contact information for help/advice in opening a club.

Make sure you have a good lawyer and a good CPA. Both will be invaluable.

I do consulting work as well as advertising.
Our business web-site is: www.AdWorksOffice.com
Some helpful hints I can write now…off the top of my head…

1. Write a business plan. Stick to your business plan. Some sections in plan should be…Cost of set up, monthly operations, daily operations, competition, expected income, job descriptions, expected growth, marketing plan…
2. Make sure you purchase a mailing list and send out postcards notifying the residents and the neighboring businesses that you will be opening soon.
3. Start a registration list and when you know it will definitely open and the date take deposits so you have a cash flow upon opening. Things come up.
4. Make sure you have a staff ready as well as a list of substitutes because staff members get sick and businesses grow.
5. Make sure the person at the front entrance is friendly and knowledgeable.
6. Make sure you have a list of emergency numbers, directions to hospitals, a telephone in the gymnastics area, two lines or a cell phone in case power goes out.
7. Make sure you have emergency telephone numbers for all of your athletes.
8. Make sure the recreational gymnasts are going to be coached by experienced, knowledgeable, and clean cut staff members.
9. Make sure you keep your club clean and safe.
10. Run safety inspections daily and weekly.
11. Have tools on hand to maintain or repair equipment.
12. Keep in mind; the recreational program pays the bills and the team program makes the reputation.

13. Make decisions based on the well-being of the athletes only.
14. Everything regarding finances looks better on paper than in real life.
15. Make sure your staff members are respectful and courteous of one another.
16. Allow the staff to improvise schedules when necessary.
17. Allow responsible staff members to suggest ideas regarding equipment.
18. Make sure there is one person in charge on each side of the wall between the gymnastics area, reception area, and office area.
19. Be at the club! Be an active owner, even after "business hours."
20. Have informal short meetings with staff members every day.

Feel free to contact me should you need more specific help rather than just a list of useful tips.

Michelle asks
Subject: booster clubs
Question: Karen, I am interested in finding out club owners benefits from a booster club. Would you be able to give me some pros and cons?
What would be the difference between a booster club and a parent organization?

Hello Michelle,

I have seen some clubs run smoother because of the help from the parents and others nearly fall apart because the parents get too involved in the business or coaching end.

The biggest benefit is that there are a lot of people to help out. They help with fund raising events, hosting competitions, and other work for the competition season such as ordering or measuring for the uniforms. They do free up the coaches and club owner's time.

At times, the parents can become too comfortable with helping the gym out and can interfere with the running of the club or the training.

So I would say it depends on the relationship of the parents to the club manager or owner. It seems that when the ground rules are set in the beginning the parent's can be a great help.

It just needs to be made clear what the purpose of the parents organization is and what the boundaries are regarding decisions, management, and coaching.

Erin R Asks
Subject: Coaches?
Question: Hello. I am a new gym club owner and I have been looking for a head coach for my girls level 4-10. I currently have 13 girls on team. I live in a small town. Do you have any suggestions on how I can find a coach? Also an idea on what type of salary range I should be offering would be helpful.

Thanks Erin

Hello Erin,

Place ads in the local newspapers, on college bulletin boards, and in the classified section on the usa-gymnastics.org site.

When coaches respond, ask them what their desired salary is. If it is reasonable and affordable, give it to them if their references check out and they seem right for the job.

Salary ranges should be appropriate for experience levels. When I had my club, the salaries ranged from $8.00 per hour to $75.00 per hour. That was in 1997.

If you are looking for full time help, you may need to figure out the cost of living in your area and then work from there. For example, find out how much it is to rent an apartment and then make sure you pay them enough to live comfortably.

Feedback...

"Thanks so much Karen! I will definitely need all the help I can get and watching others is a great way for me to learn! Thanks again!"
Meghan

"Karen, Thank you for such an immediate and knowledgeable response! You have tremendous value to offer..." John W

"Thank you very much for your fast response."
Trish

"Thank you so much! I appreciate your response." Anon

"Thanks so much. I will discuss all this with my daughter. Many points you made seem very relevant to what she's experiencing."
Lisa

About the Author

Karen Goeller has a career in gymnastics spanning over thirty years, her last twenty plus of which were spent coaching.

Her experiences include everything from team coach to gym owner, from fitness trainer to fitness researcher, and from camp director to meet director.

Karen, along with her staff, has produced NY State Champions, National TOPS Team Athletes, and Empire State Games Athletes. Most recently, Karen was a team coach at Gymnastics Training Center, MA for the Girls Level 9/10 Team.

She and her athletes have been featured regularly in the press on such national venues as Good Morning America, GoodDay NY, Eyewitness News, New York Times, NY Newsday, Brooklyn Bridge Magazine, and Interview Magazine.

Before earning her Bachelor of Arts Degree, Karen's education included training as an Emergency Medical Technician, Physical Therapist, and Nutritionist.

She has held certifications such as Nutritional Analysis, Counseling Techniques, Childcare Fundamentals, USAG Safety Certification, USAG Meet Director, and USAG Skill Evaluator.

During her employment with Paul Spadaro and Bela Karolyi, she was able to learn the dynamics of many skills which she eagerly passed on to her students. Karen was able to produce several successful level 1-10 gymnasts throughout her coaching career.

Breinigsville, PA USA
14 November 2009
227562BV00002B/42/A